# Balance

*A Choral Dialectic*
*for Unaccompanied SATB Choir*

- Secretary Michael

"Balance"
Choral Dialectic
by Secretary Michael

ISBN: 978-1-888712-38-4

# What is a Choral Dialectic?

A "choral dialectic" is a four-movement choral work (with or without instruments) in which a rational argument about any subject is battled-out musically. There's only one rule: every choral dialectic must use the following four titles for its four movements:

### 1. "PRINCIPLE"
Each dialectic begins with a statement of some sort. This will be the subject matter for the entire work. Oftentimes the statement is an ideal - an expression of how something might be in a perfect world.

### 2. "ARGUMENT"
In this movement, the "Principle" begins its journey through the meat grinder. The Argument's job is to pick apart the principle, either supporting it or challenging it.

### 3. "COUNTERARGUMENT"
In this movement, the "Principle" gets supported or challenged again, but this time from a contrasting perspective. If the previous argument was sweet, this one will probably be sour. If the previous was about abundance, this one will probably be about scarcity.

### 4. "RESOLUTION"
Now that the "Principle" has been analyzed from different angles, some sort of final understanding will have to emerge. Maybe there will be growth, a new way of being, a new way of living in the world, a new "Principle". Or maybe not.

Machinists Union Press
web: www.machinistsunion.org
email: twimfina@gmail.com

# Balance

Duration:  Less than 18 minutes

# Principle

*(from the "Balance" choral dialectic)*

Secretary Michael

♩=112  **K1**

**9** Am · D/A · Am

S

A — Keep-ing things in ba - lance so e - v'ry-one gets

T — Keep - ing ba - lance. Keep - ing ba - lance. Keep - ing

B — Keep - ing ba - lance. Keep - ing ba - lance. Keep - ing ba - lance. Keep - ing

**12** D/A · Am · D/A · Am · D/A · Am

S — *Descant* Oo _____

A — through. Keep-ing things in ba - lance is some-thing we must do. Keep-ing things in

T — ba - lance. Keep - ing ba - lance. Keep - ing ba - lance. Keep - ing

B — ba - lance. Keep - ing ba - lance. Keep - ing ba - lance. Keep - ing

18
D/A Am D/A Am D/A Am
S
A
T
B
Oo Some - thing we must
ba - lance so e - v'ry-one gets through. Keep-ing things in ba - lance is some - thing we must
ba - lance. Keep - ing ba - lance. Keep - ing ba - lance. Some - thing we must
ba - lance. Keep - ing ba - lance. Keep - ing ba - lance. Some - thing we must
25
W27
F Dm7 Gm Gm7 C C7
do. Round and round. The
do. Round and round. Round and round. The
Bicycle Bell
do. The wheels on our bike go round and round.
do. Round and round and round and round the
31
F Dm7 C C7 F
wheels on our bike go round and round, round and round. For
wheels on our bike go round and round, round and round. For
wheels on our bike go round and round and round and round.
wheels on our bike go round and round, round and round and round for

35
Dm7 Gm Gm7 C C7
S
if they do not go round and round, round and round, round and round. For
A
if they do not go round and round, round and round, round and round. For
T
If they do not go if they do not go round and round, round and round. For
B
if they do not go round and round. Round and round and round and round. For
39 F Dm7 Em
S
if they do not go round and round, we all fall down.
A
if they do not go round and round, we all fall down.
T
if they do not go if they do not go all fall down.
B
if they do not go round and round, we all fall down.
K49
45
49 Am D/A Am D/A
S
A
Keep-ing things in ba - lance so e - v'ry-one gets through.
T
Keep - ing ba - lance. Keep - ing ba - lance. Keep - ing ba - lance.
B
Keep - ing ba - lance. Keep - ing ba - lance. Keep - ing ba - lance.

**53**

Am / D/A / Am / D/A / Am / D/A

S: *Descant*
Oo_____

A: Keep-ing things in ba-lance is some-thing we must do. Keep-ing things in ba-lance so

T: Keep - ing ba - lance. Keep - ing ba - lance. Keep - ing ba - lance.

B: Keep - ing ba - lance. Keep - ing ba - lance. Keep - ing ba - lance.

**59**

Am / D/A / Am / D/A / Am

S: _____ Oo_____ Some - thing we must do._____

A: e - v'ry-one gets through. Keep-ing things in ba - lance is some - thing we must do._____

T: Keep - ing ba - lance. Keep - ing ba - lance. Some - thing we must do._____

B: Keep - ing ba - lance. Keep - ing ba - lance. Some - thing we must do._____

**66**  M67

F / Dm⁷ / Gm / Gm⁷ / C / C⁷ / F / Dm⁷

T: ____ (Move! Move! Move!) To dance a - cross the ground, (Move! Move! Move!) a

B: ____ (Move! Move! Move!) To dance a - cross the ground, (Move! Move! Move!) a

**73**

Gm     C7     F        F        Dm7

S: (Move!   Move!   Move!)   To

A: (Move!   Move!   Move!)   To

T: ba - lance must be found.   (Move!   Move!   Move!)   To

B: ba - lance must be found. We are a - mo - vin' and a - mo - vin' and a - mo - vin' and a - mo - vin' and a-

**77**

Gm     Gm7     C     C7     F        Dm7

S: dance a - cross the ground,   (Move!   Move!   Move!)   a

A: dance a - cross the ground,_____   (Move!   Move!   Move!)   a

T: dance a - cross the ground,   (Move!   Move!   Move!)   a

B: mo - vin' and a - mo - vin' and a - mo - vin' and a - mo - vin' and a - mo - vin' and a - mo - vin' and a - mo - vin' and a - mo - vin' and a

**81**

Gm     C7     F    **M83**    F        Dm7

S: ba - lance must be found. E - v'ry - bo - dy!   mo - vin' and a - mo - vin' and a - mo - vin' and a-

A: ba - lance must be found.   mo - vin' and a - mo - vin' and a - mo - vin' and a-

T: ba - lance must be found.   (Move!   Move!   Move!)   To

B: mo - vin' and a - mo - vin' be found.   mo - vin' and a - mo - vin' and a - mo - vin' and a-

85
Gm Gm7 C C7 F Dm7
S
mo-vin' and a-mo-vin' and a-mo-vin' and a-mo-vin' and a-mo-vin' and a-mo-vin' and a-mo-vin' and a-mo-vin' and a
A
mo-vin' and a-mo-vin' and a-mo-vin' and a-mo-vin' and a-mo-vin' and a-mo-vin' and a-mo-vin' and a-mo-vin' and a
T
dance a-cross the ground, (Move! Move! Move!) a
B
mo-vin' and a-mo-vin' and a-mo-vin' and a-mo-vin' and a-mo-vin' and a-mo-vin' and a-mo-vin' and a-mo-vin' and a
89
Gm C7 F
K95
95
Am D/A
S
mo-vin' and a ba-lance be found.
A
mo-vin' and a ba-lance be found. Keep-ing things in ba-lance so
T
ba-lance must be found. Keep-ing ba-lance. Keep-ing ba-lance.
B
mo-vin' and a ba-lance be found. Keep-ing ba-lance. Keep-ing ba-lance.
97
Am D/A Am D/A Am D/A
S
A
e-v'ry-one gets through. Keep-ing things in ba-lance is some-thing we must do.
T
Keep-ing ba-lance. Keep-ing ba-lance. Keep-ing ba-lance.
B
Keep-ing ba-lance. Keep-ing ba-lance. Keep-ing ba-lance.

S113

**Measure 103** (Chords: Am, D/A, Am, D/A, Am, D/A, Am)

- S (Descant): Oo_____ Oo_____ Some-thing
- A: Keep-ing things in ba - lance so e - v'ry-one gets through. Keep-ing things in ba - lance is some-thing
- T: Keep - ing ba - lance. Keep - ing ba - lance. Keep - ing ba - lance. Some-thing
- B: Keep - ing ba - lance. Keep - ing ba - lance. Keep - ing ba - lance. Some-thing

**Measure 110** (Chords: A♭, G♭)

- S: we must do._____
- A: we must do._____
- T: we must do._____ Some - where_ be-tween the two ex - tremes there is a
- B: we must do._____

**Measure 115** (Chords: A♭, G♭, A♭, G♭, A♭)

- A: We need to find.
- T: ba - lance_ we need to find. Some-where be-tween the bat-tle lines there is a ba - lance_ we need to

**B121**

120

Gb   F   Dm7   Gm   Gm7   C   C7

S: We need to mind.

T: mind. Ba-lance, ba-lance, work-ing for a ba-lance, work-ing for a peace-ful mid-dle way.

A: A mid-dle

B: Ba-lance, ba-lance, work-ing for a ba-lance, work-ing for a peace-ful mid-dle way.

125

F   Dm7   Gm   C7   F   Eb7

S: Ba-lance e-v'ry day.

A: way.

T: Ba-lance, ba-lance, work-ing for a ba-lance, work-ing for a ba-lance e-v'ry - day.____

B: Ba-lance, ba-lance, work-ing for a ba-lance, work-ing for a ba-lance e-v'ry - day.____

**S129**

129

Ab   Gb   Ab   Gb   Ab

S: Some-where be-tween the two ex-tremes there is a ba-lance we need to find. Some-where be-tween the

A: We need to find.

T: Some-where be-tween the two ex-tremes there is a ba-lance we need to find. Some-where be-tween the

B: Some-where be-tween the two ex-tremes there is a ba-lance we need to find. Some-where be-tween the

12

BW153

**148** (G♭ A♭ G♭ A♭ G♭) *Bicycle Bell*

S: find. Some-where_ be-tween the bat-tle lines there is a ba - lance_ we need to mind.

A: through. Keep-ing things in ba - lance is some-thing we must do. The

T: find, to find._ Some-where_ be-tween the bat-tle lines there is a ba - lance_ we need to mind.

B: find. Some-where_ be-tween the bat-tle lines there is a ba - lance_ we need to mind.

**153** (F Dm7 Gm Gm7 C C7)

S: Ba - lance, ba - lance, work-ing for a ba - lance, work-ing for a peace-ful mid-dle way.

A: wheels on our bike go round and round, round and round, round and round. The

T: Ba - lance, ba - lance, work-ing for a ba - lance, work-ing for a peace-ful mid-dle way.

B: Wheels on our bike go round and round. Round and round and round and round the

**157** (F Dm7 Gm C7 F C7)

S: Ba - lance, ba - lance, work-ing for a ba - lance, work-ing for a ba-lance e - v'ry - day. E - v'ry-bo - dy!

A: wheels on our bike go round and round, round and round. The

T: Ba - lance, ba - lance, work-ing for a ba - lance, work-ing for a ba-lance e - v'ry - day._

B: wheels on our bike go round and round, round and round and round._

**BWM161**

Soprano (161): Ba - lance, ba - lance, work - ing for a ba - lance, work - ing for a peace - ful mid - dle

Alto (161): wheels on our bike go round and round, round and round,

Tenor (161): (Move! Move! Move!) To dance a - cross the

Bass (161): Mo - vin' and a - mo - vin' and a - mo - vin' and a - mo - vin' and a - mo - vin' and a - mo - vin' and a -

Soprano (164): way. Ba - lance, ba - lance, work - ing for a ba - lance,

Alto (164): Round and round. The wheels on our bike go round and round,

Tenor (164): ground, (Move! Move! Move!) a

Bass (164): mo - vin' and a - mo - vin' and a - mo - vin' and a - mo - vin' and a - mo - vin' and a - mo - vin' and a -

Soprano (167): work - ing for a ba - lance e - v'ry - day. Now the end - ing! Ba - lance, ba - lance,

Alto (167): round and round. The wheels on our bike go

Tenor (167): ba - lance must be found. (Move! Move!

Bass (167): mo - vin' and a - mo - vin' and a - mo - vin' and a - mo - vin' and a - mo - vin' and a - mo - vin' and a -

**170** (Dm7 — Gm — Gm7 — C — C7)

S: work-ing for a ba-lance, work-ing for a peace-ful mid-dle way.

A: round and round, round and round, round and round. The

T: Move!) To dance a-cross the ground,

B: mo-vin' and a-mo-vin' and a-mo-vin' and a-mo-vin' and a-mo-vin' and a-mo-vin' and a-

**173** (F — Dm7 — Gm)

S: Ba-lance, ba-lance, work-ing for a ba-lance. We're work-ing for a

A: wheels on our bike go round and round and round

T: (Move! Move! Move!) a ba-lance

B: mo-vin' and a-mo-vin' and a-mo-vin' and a-mo-vin' and we mo-vin' and a-mo-vin' and a-

**176** (C — C7 — F)

S: ba-lanced mid-dle way.

A: and round.

T: must be Keep-ing things in ba-lance.

B: mo-vin' and a mov-in' mid-dle way.

# Argument

*(from the "Balance" choral dialectic)*

Secretary Michael

♩. = 36
Eb Ebm Bb Bb7 Eb Ebm Bb Bb7
T
This word we call "ba - lance" re-quires ma-ny things: re-quires that we li - mit the notes that we sing, re-
B
Ba - lance, ba - lance, ba - lance. Ba - lance, ba - lance, ba - lance.
6
Eb Ebm Bb Bb7 Eb Ebm Bb
quires we be mo - dest, re strained and sub - dued, with - out too much mo - ney and with - out too much food. With
Ba - lance, ba - lance, ba - lance. Ba - lance, ba - lance, ba - lance.
10
Eb Ebm Bb Bb7 Eb Ebm Bb Bb7
out too much sta - tus, with - out too much pride, with - out feel - ing pri - v'leged or too sa - tis - fied. This
Ba - lance, ba - lance, ba - lance. Ba - lance, ba - lance, ba - lance.
14
Eb Ebm Bb Bb7 Eb Ebm Bb
word we call "ba - lance" re - quires ma - ny things, but worth it be - cause of the peace that it brings.
Ba - lance, ba - lance, ba - lance. Ba - lance, ba - lance, ba - lance.

*Slightly slower*
♩. = 30

**18**

E♭     B♭maj7     E♭

S: This is for those who sing on one note, so o-thers are free to

A: *Tenors have center stage; Sopranos must not overpower them* — Ah_____ Ah_____

T: This is for those who sing on one note. This is for those who sing on one note, so o-thers are free to

B: Ah_____ Ah_____

♩. = 30

*Piano for rehearsal only (useful in learning dissonances)*

Ped. Ped. Ped. Ped. (etc...)

**23**

B♭     E♭     B♭maj7     E♭

S: dream and to hope. So o-thers can sing all o-ver the scale. So o-thers can rest and

A: _____ Ah_____ Ah_____

T: dream and to hope. So o-thers can sing all o-ver the scale. So o-thers can rest and

B: _____ Ah_____ Ah_____

Lyrics:

**m. 27 (S & T):** sim - ply ex - hale. This is for those who stay on one chord,___ so no one is lost, and

**m. 31 (S & T):** no one ig - nored. Faith - ful and stea - dy they drone on and on, ne - ver ap - plau - ded un

Bbm  Gb  Bbm  Eb  Gb  Ebm  N.C.  Bb

**S**

til they are gone.

**A**

**T**

til they are gone. This is my dream, this is my hope, to swal-low my song, and sing on one note.

*Bass/Baritone divisi*

**B**

This is my dream. This is my hope. Swal-low my song. Note.

♩. = 36

Eb  Ebm  Bb  Bb⁷  Eb  Ebm  Bb  Bb⁷

**T**

This word we call "ba-lance" re-quires we be strong and not fall to pie-ces when-some-thing goes wrong. For

**B**

Ba-lance, ba-lance, ba - lance. Ba-lance, ba-lance, ba - lance.

Eb  Ebm  Bb  Bb⁷  Eb  Ebm  Bb

**T**

those who can ba-lance in ter-ri-ble wea-ther will keep us con-nec-ted and keep us to-ge-ther. The

**B**

Ba-lance, ba-lance, ba - lance. Ba-lance, ba-lance, ba - lance.

**49**

*(T)* an-cient a-sce-tics once showed us a way, and ma-ny a-round us still do so to-day. To

*(B)* Ba-lance, ba-lance, ba - lance. Ba-lance, ba-lance, ba - lance.

Chords: Eb  Ebm  Bb  Bb7  Eb  Ebm  Bb  Bb7

**53**

*(T)* you who have ba-lance, you help make us whole. We thank you and ce - le-brate your self con-trol.

*(B)* Ba-lance, ba-lance, ba - lance. Ba-lance, ba-lance, ba - lance.

Chords: Eb  Ebm  Bb  Bb7  Eb  Ebm  Bb

*Slightly slower*

**57**  ♩. = 30

*(S)* This is for those___who sing on one tone,___ so o-thers can sing a

*Tenors have center stage again;*
*Sopranos must not overpower them*

*(A)* Ah_____  Ah_____

*(T)* This is for those___who sing on one tone. This is for those___who sing on one tone,___ so o-thers can sing a

*(B)* Ah_____  Ah_____

Chords: Eb  Bbmaj7  Eb

♩. = 30

*Piano for rehearsal only*
*(useful in learning dissonances)*

Ped.  Ped.  Ped.  Ped.  (etc...)

Lyrics below the staves:

Measures 62–65:
- S/T: song of their own. This is for those____who sing on one pitch,__who know up and down and
- A/B: Ah_____ Ah_____

Measures 66–69:
- S/T: know which is which. This is for those who sing in our schools,__who stay back to help their
- A/B: Ah_____ Ah_____

Chord symbols (m. 62–65): B♭  E♭  B♭maj7  E♭

Chord symbols (m. 66–69): B♭  E♭  B♭  E♭

Lyrics (measures 70–73):

S/T: stu-dents get tools.___ We ho-nor their work,___ their count-less re-frains.___ We pro-mise their work___ has

A/B: ___ Ah___ Ah___

Lyrics (measures 74–):

S: not been in vain.

T: not been in vain. This is my dream, this is my hope,___ to swal-low my song and sing on one note.

B: ___ This is my dream. This is my hope. Swal-low my song. Note.

*Bass/Baritone divisi*

# Counterargument

*(from the "Balance" choral dialectic)*

Secretary Michael

**T:** This word we call "ba-lance" re-quires ma-ny things: re-quires that we li-mit the notes that we sing, re-

**B:** Ba-lance, ba-lance, ba - lance. Ba-lance, ba-lance, ba - lance.

**T:** quires we be mo-dest, re-strained and sub-dued, with-out too much mo-ney and with-

**B:** Ba-lance, ba-lance, ba - lance. Ba-lance, ba-lance,

*Screech of Tires (non-pitched falsetto)*

*(RAP: spoken in outrage)*

**S:** Errr! Stop this song! Peo-ple preach-ing "ba-lance" seem to

**A:** Errr! Stop this song! Peo-ple preach-ing "ba-lance" seem to

**T:** out too much Errr! Who wrote this tripe?

**B:** Errr! Who wrote this tripe?

**13**

S: NE - ver get it right!

A: NE - ver get it right!

T: NE - ver get it right!
Peo - ple preach - ing "self - con - trol" and sing - ing one - note songs,

B: Peo - ple preach - ing "self - con - trol" and sing - ing one - note songs,

**16**

S: We, the ones who HAVE no ba - lance,

A: We, the ones who HAVE no ba - lance,

T: THEY're the ve - ry peo - ple seem to al - ways get it wrong!

B: THEY're the ve - ry peo - ple seem to al - ways get it wrong!

**19**

S: on the o - ther hand, we sing ALL the notes, we aren't a - fraid of be - ing grand!

A: on the o - ther hand, we sing ALL the notes, we aren't a - fraid of be - ing grand!

T:

B:

**22**

S: *(rhythmic × noteheads)*
We are not a fraid of "too much this" or "too much that"!

A: *(rhythmic × noteheads)*
We are not a fraid of "too much this" or "too much that"!

T: *(rhythmic × noteheads)*
We are not a fraid of be-ing rich or be-ing fat! We are not a fraid of "too much this" or "too much that"!

B: *(rhythmic × noteheads)*
We are not a fraid of be-ing rich or be-ing fat! We are not a fraid of "too much this" or "too much that"!

**26** ♩=100

S:
This is for those who sing all the notes. Who share all their

A: *(rest)*

T:
Who live to the full-est and sow all their oats.

B: *(rest)*

**35**

S:
bo - dy, who share all their mind.

A: *(rest)*

T:
Who share all their per - son for all of man - kind.

B: *(rest)*

**42**

S: This is for those____ who sing all the notes.

*(Slide seamlessly from high soprano to low bass via soprano decrescendo and bass crescendo during slide)*

B: This is for those____ who sing all the notes.

*(If only one or several basses can sing these low notes, then the number of sopranos should be reduced to balance them)*

**50**

Bb    F    Bb⁷    Eb    Bb

S: This is for those____ who sing all the notes,____ who live to the

A: This is for those____ who sing all the notes,____ who live to the

T: This__ is__ for__ those who sing__ all__ the__ notes, who live__ to__ the__

B: This is for those____ who sing all the notes,____ who live to the

**55**

Gm⁶    Cm⁷    F⁷    Bb    F

S: full - est and sow all their oats.____ Who sing soft and loud,____ who

A: full - est and sow all their oats.____ Who sing soft and loud,____ who

T: full - est__ and sow__ all__ their__ oats. Who sing__ soft__ and__ loud, who

B: full - est and sow all their oats._____ Who__ sing soft and loud,____ who sing low and high,_ who sing out of key and then laugh and then cry.

This is for those_____ who say what they think,_ who re - cog - nize

stran - gers and give them a wink._ Who share all their bo - dy, who

**SLOWER, DECLARATORY**

share all their mind,___ who share all their per-son for all of man-kind.

share all their mind,___ who share all their per-son for all of man-kind.

share all their mind, who share all their per-son for all of man-kind.

share all their mind,___ who share all their per-son for all of man-kind.

This is my dream.___ These are my hopes:___ to

This is my dream.___ These are my hopes:___ to

This is my dream. These are my hopes: to

This is my dream.___ These are my hopes:___ to

swal-low my song___ and sing all the notes.

swal-low my song___ and sing all the notes.

swal-low my song and sing all the notes.

swal-low my song___ and sing all the notes.

RESUME TEMPO

**90**

S: This is for those___ who sing all the notes.

*(Slide seamlessly from high soprano to low bass via soprano decrescendo and bass crescendo during slide)*

*(If only one or several basses can sing these low notes, then the number of sopranos should be reduced to balance them)*

B: This is for those___ who sing all the notes.

**98**

Bb      F      Bb7      Eb      Bb

S: This is for those___ who are not a - fraid___ to live e - v'ry

A: This is for those___ who are not a - fraid___ to live e - v'ry

T: This___ is___ for___ those who are___ not a - fraid to live___ e - v'ry___

B: This is for those___ who are not a - fraid___ to live e - v'ry

**103**

Gm6      Cm7      F7      Bb      F

S: day in a march - ing pa - rade.___ To dance and to dance and to

A: day in a march - ing pa - rade.___ To dance and to dance and to

T: day___ in a___ march - ing___ pa - rade. To dance and___ to___ dance, to

B: day in a march - ing pa - rade.___ To dance and to dance and to

**108** (Bb7 / Eb / Bb / F / Ebm / Bb)

S: dance 'til con - vul-sive and ne - ver to fear the ob - ses - sive com - pul-sive.

A: dance 'til con - vul-sive and ne - ver to fear the ob - ses - sive com - pul-sive.

T: dance 'til con - vul-sive and ne - ver to fear the ob - ses - sive com - pul-sive.

B: dance 'til con - vul-sive and ne - ver to fear the ob - ses - sive com - pul-sive.

**114** (F / F7 / Bb / Eb)

S: This is for those who sing all the notes with u - vu - las

A: This is for those who sing all the notes with u - vu - las

T: This is for those who sing all the notes with u - vu - las

B: This is for those who sing all the notes with u - vu - las

**119** (C / F / F7 / Bb / Fm)

S: flap - ping in all of their throats. Who sing it out loud and

A: flap - ping in all of their throats. Who sing it out loud and

T: flap - ping in all of their throats. Who sing it out loud and

B: flap - ping in all of their throats. Who sing it out loud and

**SLOWER, DECLARATORY**

sing it out fast and sing it with joy as if it were their last.

This is my dream. These are my hopes: to

swal - low my song and sing all the notes.

# Resolution

*(from the "Balance" choral dialectic)*

Secretary Michael

Lyrics (Alto, mm. 1–4): Should we just hum one tone?_
Lyrics (Soprano, Alto, Tenor, Bass, mm. 3–4): Or sing a sym - pho - ny?

Lyrics (Alto, mm. 5–8): Whis - per it all a - lone?_
Lyrics (Soprano, mm. 7–8): Or join in har - mo - ny? A
Lyrics (Alto, Tenor, Bass, mm. 7–8): Or join in har - mo - ny?

Measure 9

**Chords:** B♭ · D⁷ · Gm · Gm⁷ · B♭⁷

**S:** "ba- lanced life"_ is what we_ sing,_ but "ba-lanced life" for you may be a dif- frent thing. For

**A:** "ba- lanced life"_ is what we_ sing,_ but "ba-lanced life" for you may be a dif- frent thing. For

**T:** "ba- lanced life"_ is what we_ sing,_ but "ba-lanced life" for you may be a dif- frent thing.

**B:** "ba- lanced life"_ is what we_ sing,_ but "ba-lanced life" for you may be a dif- frent thing.

Measure 13

**Chords:** E♭ · F⁷ · B♭ · D⁷ · Gm · Gm⁷

**S:** who is ba- lanced, who is not for us to__ say.__ The

**A:** who is ba- lanced, who is not for us to__ say.__ The

**T:** Who, who is not is not for us to__ say.__ The

**B:** Who, who is not is not for us to__ say.__ The

Measure 17

**Chords:** E♭ · C · E♭m · F⁷

**S:** ones who sing from dif- frent_ scores will sing them a dif frent_ way.__ Some

**A:** ones who sing from dif- frent_ scores will sing them a dif frent_ way.__ Some

**T:** ones who sing from dif- frent_ scores will sing them a dif frent_ way.__

**B:** ones who sing from dif- frent_ scores will sing them a dif frent, dif - frent way.

21
B♭
D7
Gm
Gm7
B♭7
S
sing what they want, some o-thers re- sist,_ for some a "ba-lanced life" doe-sn't e-ven ex-ist._ Some
A
sing what they want, some o-thers re- sist,_ for some a "ba-lanced life" doe-sn't e-ven ex-ist._ Some
T
Sing what they want, some o-thers re- sist,_ for some a "ba-lanced life" doe-sn't e-ven ex-ist._
B
Sing what they want, some o-thers re- sist,_ for some a "ba-lanced life" doe-sn't e-ven ex-ist._
25
E♭
F7
B♭
D7
Gm
Gm7
S
croon and wail, some cry some sing from Car-ne-gie Hall._ But
A
croon and wail, some cry some sing from Car-ne-gie Hall._ But
T
Croon, cry from jail, some sing from Car-ne-gie Hall._ But
B
Croon, cry from jail, some sing from Car-ne-gie Hall._ But
29
E♭
C
E♭m
F7
S
if we_ want_ a ba- lanced life,_ we've got to learn to sing them all._ We
A
if we_ want_ a ba- lanced life,_ we've got to learn to sing them all._ We
T
if we_ want_ a ba- lanced life,_ we've got to learn to sing them all._
B
if we_ want_ a ba- lanced life,_ we've got to learn to sing them sing_ them all.

Measures 33–36:

lis-ten and learn as best as we can___ so we can sing the song of e-v'ry wo-man and man. We

Measures 37–40:

chant with the monks, we share in their bread,___ go ca-rol-ing with San-ta and go rid-ing on his sled. We

Measures 41–44:

soar with the di - vas,___ we wail with the blues. We join the town cri-er to pro-claim the___ news: We're

*(Altos and Basses in unison with opening theme from Credo)*

**S** (m. 45): keep-ing things in ba - lance. We're keep-ing things in ba - lance. We're

**A**: keep-ing things in ba - lance, we're keep-ing things in ba - lance, we're

**T**: keep-ing things in ba - lance, we're keep-ing things in ba - lance, we're

**B**: keep-ing things in ba - lance, we're keep-ing things in ba - lance, we're

**S** (m. 49): keep-ing things in ba - lance, so e - v'ry - one gets through.____

**A**: keep-ing things in ba - lance, so e - v'ry - one gets through.____

**T**: keep-ing things in ba - lance, so e - v'ry - one gets through.____

**B**: keep-ing things in ba - lance, so e - v'ry - one gets through.____

## CREDO

K
Keeping things in balance so ev'ryone gets through
Keeping things in balance is something we must do

_____

W
The wheels on our bike go round and round
Round and round, round and round
The wheels on our bike go round and round
Round and round

For if they do not go round and round
Round and round, round and round
For if they do not go round and round
We all fall down

_____

M
(Move, move, move)
To dance across the ground
(Move, move, move)
A balance must be found

_____

S
Somewhere between the two extremes
There is a balance we need to find (we need to find)
Somewhere, between the battle lines
There is a balance we need to mind (we need to mind)

_____

B
Balance, balance, working for a balance
Working for a peaceful middle way
Balance, balance, working for a balance
Working for a balance ev'ry day.

_____

## ONE HAND

This word we call "balance" requires many things
Requires that we limit the notes that we sing
Requires we be modest, restrained and subdued
Without too much money and without too much food

Without too much status, without too much pride
Without feeling privileged or too satisfied
This word we call "balance" requires many things
But worth it because of the peace that it brings

_____

This is for those who sing on one note
So others are free to dream and to hope
So others can sing all over the scale
So others can rest and simply exhale

This is for those who stay on one chord
So no one is lost, and no one ignored
Faithful and steady they drone on and on
Never applauded until they are gone

This is my dream, this is my hope
To swallow my song – and sing on one note

_____

This word we call "balance" requires we be strong
And not fall to pieces when something goes wrong
For those who can balance in terrible weather
Will keep us connected and keep us together

The ancient ascetics once showed us a way
And many around us still do so today
To you who have balance, you help make us whole
We thank you and celebrate your self-control

_____

This is for those who sing on one tone
So others can sing a song of their own
This is for those who sing on one pitch
Who know up and down, and know which is which

This is for those who sing in our schools
Who stay back to help their students get tools
We honor their work, their countless refrains
We promise their work has not been in vain

This is my dream, this is my hope
To swallow my song – and sing on one note

## OTHER HAND

This word we call "balance" requires many things
Requires that we limit the notes that we sing
Requires we be modest, restrained and subdued
Without too much money and without too much
(sound of tires screeching)

------------------------------------------------

Stop this song! Who wrote this tripe?
People preaching "balance" seem to NEVER get it
right!
People preaching "self-control" and singing one-note
songs
They're the very people seem to ALWAYS get it
wrong!

We, the ones who HAVE no balance, on the other
hand,
We sing ALL the notes, we aren't afraid of being
grand
We are not afraid of being rich or being fat!
We are not afraid of "too much this" or "too much
that".

------------------------------------------------

This is for those who sing all the notes
Who live to the fullest and sow all their oats
Who sing soft and loud, who sing low and high
Who sing out of key and then laugh and then cry

This is for those who say what they think
Who recognize strangers and give them a wink
Who share all their body, who share all their mind
Who share all their person for all of mankind

This is my dream, these are my hopes,
To swallow my song and sing all the notes

------------------------------------------------

This is for those who are not afraid
To live every day in a marching parade
To dance and to dance and to dance 'til convulsive
And never to fear the obsessive compulsive

This is for those who sing all the notes
With uvulas flapping in all of their throats
Who sing it out loud and sing it out fast
And sing it with joy as if it were their last

This is my dream, these are my hopes:
To swallow my song and sing all the notes

## GO AND DO

Should we just hum one tone? Or sing a symphony?
Whisper it all alone? Or join in harmony?

A "balanced life" is what we sing
But "balanced life" for you may be a diff'rent thing
For who is balanced, who is not, is not for us to say
The ones who sing from diff'rent scores will sing them a
diff'rent way

Some sing what they want, some others resist
For some a "balanced life" doesn't even exist.
Some croon and wail, some cry from jail, some sing from
Carnegie Hall
But if we want a balanced life, we've got to learn to sing
them all.

We listen and learn as best as we can
So we can sing the song of ev'ry woman and man

We chant with the monks, we share in their bread
Go caroling with Santa and go riding on his sled
We soar with the divas, we wail with the blues
We join the town crier to proclaim the news:

We're keeping things in balance
We're keeping things in balance
We're keeping things in balance
So ev'ryone gets through

# Recent Works by Secretary Michael

## Jo Puma - Wild Choir Music

Collection of 36 traditional "Sacred Harp" arrangements with new secular lyrics for our diverse society. This collection has removed the 3 barriers that have kept this music out of our schools: inappropriate lyrics, poor shape-note legibility, and nonstandard use of standard solfege names. Now we all have a chance to experience this exciting early American music. (Book available; check for free download: www.machinistsunion.org/works.html)

## Secular Hymnal

Collection of 144 favorite hymn tunes from around the world. The hymn tunes have been re-notated and given thoughtful egalitarian lyrics that promote peace. Many public schools use them for choral sight-reading practice. Available in both unison/guitar and SATB choir editions. Now we all have a chance to share in these musical treasures. (Books available; check for free download: www.machinistsunion.org/works.html)

## Twimfina

A peace-themed musical play for singing groups of all ages. The story is about a young woman named "Twimfina" (an acronym for "The World Is My Family, I'm Not Afraid") who runs off to a hostile country. It is scored for voice and piano. The play is divided into 21 segments, many of which can stand alone. This allows an acting group to perform individual segments instead of the entire 2.5 hour play. (Book available; check for free download: www.machinistsunion.org/works.html)

## Choral Dialectics

A "choral dialectic" is a 4-movement choral work (with or without instruments) in which a rational argument is battled-out musically. There's only one rule: every choral dialectic must use the following four titles for its four movements: "Principle" - "Argument" - "Counterargument" - "Resolution"
Secretary Michael has begun working on a series of 6 choral dialectics, some of which are available now; the rest will become available as they are completed in future years. (Books available; check for free downloads: www.machinistsunion.org/works.html)

## Aren't We the Lucky Ones

A book-length story about a group of college science students who share an understanding that people don't truly have a free will. There are no "good people" or "bad people", just lucky and unlucky ones. This insight carries with it the responsibility to protect the "unlucky" from the wrath of the "lucky". The students form a community in order to live out their ideals. (Book available - both paperback and digital).

## Joy of Piggyback Songs

Dozens of fun, short choral works in which more than one melody is sung at the same time. Book (and free internet download) will become available after it is completed.

*"Please help create public choirs that are free from religious and nationalistic content so that all singers feel welcome."*

*- Secretary Michael*